THE RESURRECTION MACHINE

With surgical precision, Steve Gehrke's poems open us to the complex mysteries of our fragmented bodies and lives. What happens inside us when a mother's donated kidney fails inside her son? What does this world look like to a man pacing in autism's villanelle? How does a marriage weather a husband's genuine doubts about how he'll feel toward his wife when another person's heart beats in his chest? Thousands of patients literally own what this poet calls "fractions of the dead." All of us do, metaphorically. These are eerie salvations, the chances offered by medical science and by poetry. Gehrke guides us, with hand-stitched wisdom, through suffering and toward a healing that requires giving thanks for what others have given so that we might live.

—*Peggy Shumaker*

Steve Gehrke's poems chronicle the body's losses and recoveries. *The Resurrection Machine* is a fearless investigation of both the world of the body and the body of the world. In this book, the poems offer us a profoundly moving evocation of illness, death, and a surprising and redemptive faith, while their musicality engages and delights us. A heart "opens and closes like a dark umbrella." A man "unlock[s]" himself from his own skin. The body's organs divide the past from the future. The poems in this collection introduce us to a daring and eloquent new voice in American poetry.

—*Nicole Cooley*

THE RESURRECTION MACHINE

poems

Steve Gehrke

John Ciardi Prize for Poetry Winner
Selected by Miller Williams

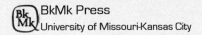 BkMk Press
University of Missouri-Kansas City

BkMk Press
University of Missouri-Kansas City
5100 Rockhill Road
Kansas City, Missouri 64110
(816) 235-2558
bkmk@umkc.edu
www.umkc.edu/bkmk

BkMk Press conducts the John Ciardi Prize for Poetry
competition to select the best full-length poetry manuscript
submitted by a living author and written in English.
For more information, contact BkMk Press.

Cover design for second printing: Chelsea Seguin
Cover photographs: Chelsea Seguin & Susan L. Schurman

Library of Congress Cataloguing-in-Publication Data
Gehrke, Steve
   The resurrection machine : poems / Steve Gehrke.
     p. cm.
     ISBN 1-886157-21-9
     1. Physically handicapped—Poetry.
     2. Body, Human—Poetry.
     I. Title.
     PS3557.E3549 R47 2000
     813'.54—dc21   00-023637
                           CIP

CONTENTS

IV

What I like most about the poems of Steve Gehrke is that while they're finished, they're not complete. There's always something left undone for me to do, so that when I've read one I feel like I've been inside of it with him. Making this possible takes both skill and what I want to call an amiability on the part of the poet—the willingness to invite a reader in, and the skill to leave room for that. It makes the reading a joy.

—*Miller Williams*
Judge, John Ciardi Prize for Poetry

Acknowledgments

Special thanks to Kathy Murphy, Edward Micus, Roger Sheffer, Rick Robbins, Dick Terrill, Cynthia Hogue, Nicole Cooley, and Tess Gallagher, whose guidance helped to craft these poems.

Grateful acknowledgment is made to the editors of the following publications where poems in this book have appeared:

American Poetry: The Next Generation (Carnegie Mellon University Press): "Mouth to Mouth," "Near the Mississippi," "Walking Fields at Night South of Hampton, Iowa"

Black Bear Review: "Near the Mississippi"

Borderlands: Texas Poetry Review: "Chronic Fatigue Syndrome," "Moon with Bells," "Six Weeks Before You Died"

Chiron Review: "Walter Mondale at McDonald's"

Comstock Review: "It Happens Like This"

Defined Providence: "November Hunters"

Mankato Poetry Review: "Dialysis," "Winter Farm," "The Sweater"

Midwest Quarterly: "Walking Fields at Night, South of Hampton, Iowa"

Passages North: "My Grandmother's False Teeth"; "The Romanian Poet"

Spillway: "Sweet Williams"

South Dakota Review: "Non-Verbal Autistic Man"

For my sister, Gwen,
With love and gratitude

I

Non-Verbal Autistic Man
For Douglas

Arrows in the carpet mark where his feet go,
the imprint of his orthopedic shoes,
from the kitchen to his bedroom window.

A hundred times a day he walks that loop,
tracing the same grooves, filling the same blue
arrows. In the carpet, his feet echo

that single note his mind is stuck on,
his knees a refrain of ups and downs.
From the kitchen to his bedroom window,

he's a factory of steps—a valve opens
in his heart and a foot lifts, then closes
and his shoe marks the carpet with an arrow.

He's repeating the one sentence he knows,
his feet typing it over and over:
This is my kitchen, my bedroom window.

Einstein said that time is hooked to motion.
In Doug, the minutes advance and withdraw.
Arrows in the carpet mark what his feet know
from the kitchen to the bedroom window.

Chronic Fatigue Syndrome

Tonight, as she writes at her desk, her mind
is a room, emptied of its furniture,

dimples in the carpet where her thoughts had been.
Her weather-less body holds onto its skin,

to its bones, those instruments of sadness,
locked in their cases.

Outside, stars pin the night in place,
rigged and haunted by their own light.

For so long, she's been trying to write,
to feel words weighing down her body,

or to walk into the past,
where the Iowa River washes through her girlhood,

her feet rooted in the riverbank's mud, hair damp
and braided by the sunlight.

Tonight, each stone that burdened her pockets
is a knot removed from her neck.

The sky is so cleaned of noise, she thinks
one right word might tap a star loose.

Give up, give up her breath says. Her heart
opens and closes like a dark umbrella.

It makes little difference what it shuts in
or what it lets go. Her own cells double,

they rearrange themselves, as her mind fills
and empties, that terrible draftiness,

as her hands begin to flutter
like the severed wings of angels.

Two Comas

In a small room, just beyond the sleep-house
with its constant arrivals and departures,

two women lie, not dead, but taking leave,
retired from consciousness,

from jobs, children, ordinary husbands,
the rituals of sex.

Morning rubdown, nurses stretching arms
and legs, they jog lying down.

They are fed together, the rain from a small storm
dripping into their veins.

With no curtain between them, bladders and bowels
draining, doctors graph their tides, and nurses

lean over their beds with basins of water
and rags until no place on them is not clean.

They are so lovely then, you would lie between them.
This far from the bully-eyes of husbands,

their faces blush with laziness. Language is nothing
to them. They breathe each other's silence.

Touch is useless. They take the emptiness
of our universe into their lungs.

There are things they do together
that we will never know.

They sleep with the dark juice
of never waking on their tongues.

Six Weeks Before You Died

In New Mexico,
we walk into a canyon of horses,
honeysuckle and loss,
a fluttering congregation of wrens.
This far from the chaos
of roads, we can almost forget
the disease that has stood up inside you.

Horses strip dry twigs for play.
You take a stick and throw it
as far as you can
as if to say, *this is my future.*
In the dip of light,
a horse stomps dust
into his fetlock
and I search the bramble for words. . .

There is no word
for the hunger cry of wren
or a horse's whinny rising
from the deep stables of longing.
Only our boot prints blending
in the sand, altering the shape of the dust
in the decaying air.

Because She Had No Children

Not a month after the tumors
started hatching in her chest,
she brings home twelve smelts,
a cargo of mercury, clapping fins
inside a pail.

She snips out the polluted artery
under the gills, and probes for tiny bones
wired through the muscles, tweezing
them out with circuit cutters.
Like a little autopsy, she thinks.

She could string their twelve hearts
into a necklace, make a dozen sets
of earrings with the eyes.
When animals die, they pass into us.

Which is what she wants:
to have her muscles
filleted, dipped in a batter,
and served with a marinade.
To be digested, her blood washing
through another heart.

My Mother at Secretarial School, 1967

Now is the time for all young mothers
to jump to the aid of their children,
     they type, the keys
       marking nownownow
   on the page. Their fingers are the players
    in a comedy: they fumble and twist on each typewriter's
       little stage. At the end, tin voices
   cling their refrains, like timers announcing
                   supper's done.
  In their uniforms and hair-pins,
     these twelve mothers-in-training,
       could be an out-of-work chorus-line, a cargo
    of goodnight kisses
  on their blackberry lips. This not-yet son
      wanders the rows, unable to choose,
    for width of grin
      or grace, whose body
          to climb into, which face
       contains the half-ghost of my face.
  I'm no speck in the ink
   of my mother's Indian
       eyes, nor the breeze between her fingers
      as they whir across the keys.
Better to watch each letter
    grip the page, upright
      and seamlessly jointed, the proud stance
    of an *A*, dip and
        slide of a *u* or *j*, and the *I*,
         with its own address,
      orphaned and unafraid.

Mouth to Mouth

Like trying to blow a feather
from the bottom of a hat,
the trickiest of negotiations.
What voice do we use
to call back the freshly dead?

My mother brought one up once.
Weighted down with airplane tequila
and flopping from the aftershocks
of a seizure, he was a real bottom-dweller,
bobbed in the battle, surfaced and dove.

She breathed into him with wind
from the storm of three small children,
troubled-marriage wind. She pressed
the rhythm of her working-mother
days into his chest.

When the living mate with the dead
it's not charity, but a balance
and counterbalance that pilfers loss-heavy coins
from the purse of each chest.

So on a day that was not Easter,
it was Easter for an average man from Ohio:
tailor, divorcé, ordinary sinner. My mother
inhaled just enough of him
so they both hovered above the rim
to the deep-hatted other world.

Moon with Bells
(After Plath)

Atheist moon, she rings bells
for nobody. Twelve strict notes,
hollowing the cold,
rattle breath from the sky,
chiming out a funeral of hours.

In 1976, my dead uncle's legs vanished
into a dark half-cave
where bats hung their inverted sleep
between his knees, and a very small wind
swished in his trousers. His face was no moon.
It was a baseball:
tiny stitching kept his neck and chin on straight.

My cousins and I
skipped pebbles into the hole.
We played hide-and-seek
behind the headstones,
a resurrection game,
each putting on the gray face
we'd live to know another way—
boyhood looses its grip
and heaven, at best,
is the passage into memory.

Because the moon has no light
of her own, she wants to remember
everything we say. I'd put a hat on her.
She is bald as a monk,
full of self-importance and terribly busy.

One-Legged Man

In the bath tub he feels it, or its weight
about to break through the surface
the way his wife raises hers to shave.
He flexes his hip muscle, and runs
the cloth over the tunnel of air where it would be.

He'd buy a wooden one if they weren't so glossy
and mechanical as if it were a privilege
to have a false leg. Maybe he'll carve one himself,
something primitive out of oak
with splinters and long cracks down the side.
Hell, maybe he'll leave the bark on.

Really he never liked walking—
to the bank, the liquor store, carrying groceries
in from the car, loads of laundry
from the basement. All this his wife does now.

He didn't lose it in the war, saving an old lady
from a mugging, gambling debts,
or passing out naked in the snow.
It's always disappointing to say *bone cancer*
when someone asks him how. Once he said
gangrene without knowing what it meant.

The Sweater

In November, when the family of tumors
decided it would stay in his chest,
the roots uncoiling in his lungs
until flesh and disease embraced,
he told his wife not to buy him any Christmas gifts,
and she put the sweater that she'd been
working on away, having finished
just one arm and a piece of the collar.

By Thanksgiving, the pump between his ribs
drained four liters a day, and still the air
had to argue its way in. When she could
no longer sleep through the pump's
watery babble, she took the sweater down,
and her hands became a tumble
of furious gestures. The hooks blurred between fingers,
balls of string thinning out on her lap.

When she gave it to him, three weeks
short of New Year's, he pulled
the sweater over his head. The pump's
catheter wormed through the collar,
and drained the river of his voice.

Note to John From a Grove Near Salisbury

August brings a fever of moths,
tender as thought, and dizzy
in the wind. Chestnut and silver fir
strip themselves of leaves: each
saddle of branches turns
to a calamity of fluttering hands.

I hear your father's dying,
the cancer bell is ringing
in his lungs. Friend,
we resent stones
for their blind honesty.
We resent the false fire
in trees that tumbles off in winter
when we really need it.

Nights here, stars harden above
the orchard. They hang out
their light. I resent their resolve
an hour, then walk home,
drawing in and turning loose the air.

II

Three Doctors
(After Ted Kooser)

Each morning they surround my chart,
their starched white coats falling to their hips
from the weight of a stethoscope or fist

in the pocket, young men whose fingers
play casually over my records, circling *high creatinine*
in black, *low white count* in red,

cataloguing medication in pencil
while they murmur to each other, not intending
for me to hear their confusion, not knowing how

listless their voices are as they yawn back and forth,
whispering their troubled kidney secrets,
their pills-up, liquids-down, dialysis lamentation.

Only once, when they were angry with each other
did their throats rattle, lips draining their faces
of color, voices shredding into breathy fragments.

Then, looking up, seeing I was watching,
they stepped cautiously to the hall.

Dialysis

When my stomach floods
like a basement, and breath
strings out slow and thick,
I drive to the clinic and lie
in a blue Lazy Boy, draining.

Nurses feed me ice-chips,
cover me with heated blankets,
and I feel a pull in the blood
as if my organs are liquid.

Little currents shift through my body,
sometimes even gravity washes
and I unlock myself from skin,
soaking up light, merging with walls.

Always I pinwheel back to myself,
drop lazy and long,
and relive my leap from Memorial Bridge
to the Minnesota River, swallowing

blades of air, spitting bile,
peeling a thousand layers of myself from wind,
something Picasso would paint,
water pushed through a wave.

Rocky

Rocky and Mickey argue with a door between them,
ghost punches in their voices, their blood making
its deliveries, a bit of temper dropped under the eyes.

Mickey fusses with his hat, says, "I'm seventy-
six years old, Rock. Seventy-six." Says it
like a surrender, a falling to the mat,
his gloved hand slipping from the bottom rope.

You're twenty-six, wake some mornings thinking
how our bodies abandon us, the referee waves
his hand once over our head and we disappear.
How do you answer the bell of the living?

You think of Rocky's muscles, tight with nerves, shoulders
blooming, pink lungs. And Mickey,
on the other side of the door we all come to,
four limbs sagging, broth in his veins, body taking
a standing eight count, while both their punching-
bag hearts keep boxing in their little rings.

My Grandmother's False Teeth

When she pulled them from her mouth,
it was a miracle of separation. They clattered
and sank into a glass of water, displacing some.
She sailed her tongue along the damp
peach-halves of her gums, and curled her lips
into her mouth, as if relishing the last
dark drink of something sweet and missing.

From the breathless teeth, I looked
to her face, waiting for her to unscrew
a finger, an eye to pirouette from its socket,
wondering if there were hidden seams
in bodies, if they could be taken apart
and patched back in place.

Now, when my sister has given up
her kidney, when it has been cut from her
body and laced into mine, I think
of that afternoon in Grandmother's
kitchen, the empty dish of her mouth,
and how when she spoke it was like her words
were swimming armless from her face,
the underwater moan of a women telling her grandson
there was nothing to be afraid of.

Gift

This is what
I will call you: Extra
baggage. Armless fist
with a thousand
busy mouths. Little
refinery. Pocket of
my thirst. Stone
dividing past
from future. Bell
of the man
I am becoming.

You are
the inspector
at the end of the river,
filtering the lethal
from the clean.
Everything
that drains
from you
is gold.

News Item:
Man Receives First Hand Transplant

I.
Even before surgery, the patient decided
the donor was a PBA bowler, fingers thick from nachos
and beer, that he'd had children, a young
wife, a mistress who followed him
on tour. That a heart-attack failed
to topple him, but a stroke
picked up the spare, and in the ICU
the doctor noticed the donor's muscular
wrist, tendons strengthened
from the three-finger grip, skin on the palm
kept smooth with talcum powder.

The patient imagined the hand's
history of touches: black marble, breaded
onion rings, heat from the candles
the bowler, then a young altar boy, lit.
And even earlier, a pencil
tense between his fingers
from the stress of imagining fractions.

II.
There are thousands of us who own
fractions of the dead: kidneys,
livers, hearts, corneas, lungs and one
new hand, waving away paradise.
We are not superhuman
but not less than human. Not dead, but not
not-dead. We are imaginary as fractions,
the simple arithmetic of us divided by them.

Our bodies are repaired with metallic
instruments, microscopes and catheters,
dialysis units and bags of clear
fluid, magnetic plates and clamps,
heart monitors and pacemakers,
little paper cups of pills, needles, sponges,
suction hoses and scalpels—
the resurrection machine.

III.
In a dream, the patient rolls strike after strike,
the pins colliding, a bowling glove
like a tiny jacket for his hand,
which he raises after every strike,
locked into a fist, as if holding on
to one-half of a prayer.
In his dream, the ambitious doctor sees
thousands of confused bodies,
mistakenly numbering them one
and one and one and one. . . .

IV.
After the surgery—when a T-plate
bridge had connected bone
to bone, a path for the touches
to ride home, the veins laced
together with stitches so small they could join
two grains of sand—the hand blushed with color,
the blood's new piping warming
the fingers, the strung-together tendons

already repairing themselves, as they wheeled
the patient into the hallway, leaving the O.R.
dark and empty as a cave.

Heart Transplants

Tonight, I'm thinking of the men
who trade in their hearts,
of the lonely woman with a man heart,
the Jew with a Muslim heart,
and the man who said to his wife
on the morning of surgery, "I don't know
if I will love you when I wake up."

What I love is how each of them
was willing to fall asleep
and wake to the tapping
of a new message, how they eased
into another heart, filling it
with their own fluids, their own breath,
how their ribs unlocked
and the purse of each chest
accepted the alien shape.

The man still loves his wife,
though he takes down
all the mirrors in the house.
The Jew still fears Allah.
Some nights, he dreams Muslims
hold his old heart hostage,
and force it to convert.

Every night from her house
the woman watches dusk
burn through her windows
and feels a soft typing against her chest,
a pushing out and falling away,
I love you. I am dead.

III

High Dive

Something in the sun-blurred
paper-faces below
turns you acrobat,
and you leap, arms
flywheel, in a fistfight
with gravity.

Midair, others fall
around you, some reaching
for invisible safety ropes.
What plane or god
has dropped them?
What wind blew apart
the clouds they stood on?

When you sliver
through, you don't ask forgiveness
from the broken water. It's deeper,
heavier than you. It makes little
difference if you drown,
your last breath bubbling up
rosary beads.

The next in line still sees you
rebound to the surface,
your face a scrap of paper
with this between the margins:
jump,
         it is terrible,
it is not so bad.

Sweet Williams

All day they purple.
All day the sweetness
loosens in their bellies.
Hunched on their backbones,
purple-hatted churchgoers,
every petal hides a fragrance
in the bloodwork of its skin.
The sun will not wilt them,
the sky will not carry them away.
For their blossoming,
even the wind trembles.
Underground, a hand of roots
spreads fingerholds against
the wintering of the world.
And that scent, like heartwood,
rising in the wind? Isn't that
the world silently burning,
what we've come to live for?

The Language of Dreams

Gibberish or the curved truth of stones?
A small noise: weeds sharpening
each other in the wind, or the mind
clicking in its box of gears?

The tumble-blush of fall
becomes the dreaming season, trees
undressing like multitudes of women
removing a million glittering earrings.

When we sleep, the drowsy unconscious
murmurs awake, the current rises
to the top of the river, whirling the water
into the soothing voice of stars, stars, stars....

What Can I Say About Hands?

That they are there, dangling,
fingers in their numbered pouches,
palms grooved and dented?

If the spine is a tree
fingers are the ends of its roots.

If the heart is a kitchen,
boiling its toxins,
hands are the last to be fed.

The world spins,
a factory of textiles,
and the hands latch, unlatch,
sift and rub.

The mind clicks them open
and closed. They collect
little touches, wiring
them home, and the mind
thanks them with feeling.

Freedom, Nevada

A stitch of mountains trims the horizon.
The wind discovers its gears
and aims for ground the prison was built on.
Inmates slide down the hill on trains.
The moon drops its yellow anchor in the sand
and the cars are unbuckled in pairs.

Shrubs hold out a braid of limbs for rain.
Pheasants arrive on schedule from all points north
coupled with the currents that leave them here.
The hotel that names this town went broke
from the bankers' lien. From deep
in the prison's intestines, voices fashion a song

while the pheasants test the air for south.
Their wings flag this town. One, crime. One, drought.

Beehive

I don't know how bees
remember the airy path
to the nectar puddles
or how the flowers know
it's spring and time to blaze open
from a fist of dreams.

I know there is logic,
so why are we so willing
to overlook the flaws
in death—its randomness,
the stubborn way it points
its finger, how it reaches
with one hand into our chests?

From a factory of honey, the bees
float into the world, wheeling
from petal to petal,
swirling blindly through the thistles.
They don't ask where
they are going, or who the pilot is.

It Happens Like This

One morning, you wake early
to a fluttering in your chest,
your heart flapping its wings,
lifting your dead-weight bones
from bed. You stand at the window
of your slippered life and watch
the sun slide from the darkness,
dropping its bright twigs into
the distant fields. Clouds inflate
with light, as if they'd been
sleeping above you all night
in black beds of air. The grass
stretches its back; frost burns away
until the yard becomes a harbor
of green light. Peonies unfold
the pages of their petals, and the bright red
handkerchief that drops into the branches
is a cardinal. You see the look
of distance and amazement on your
own face reflected in the glass,
how you are beginning to love this world.

Near the Mississippi

August stretches into fall. Clouds spread
rumors of a false frontier. Above you,
the moon raises a fist at the stars.

A shudder of dust blurs the highway
and you realize for the hundredth
time that you have never existed,

that the river braids two thousand hard
miles south and never breaks its spine,
that trees are the bones in the perfect

anatomy of a forest, and that stems,
goldenrod say, can stitch themselves
in the same pinholes of earth for years

and never need rain or shade.
They are complete in their delicate bodies.
And you, in a crude garment of skin, are not.

Crows, Frozen in the Snow

Follow 61 south, past Selinsgrove,
to where the shoulders fall from the sides of the road.
Through the trees, and down that slope,
a gang of crows, gone dumb with cold.

Some storm has torn the roofs right off their skulls,
blown apart their wings' upholstery.
Though they died here, feathers a smattering
of oil on snow, applaud the storm that kills,

and forty miles south burns out, trailing smoke.
Look at the muscular stones, the bully clouds,
a willow, drunk on storm, and applaud
when the wind is open. When it's closed,

your heart quells its own tumble of crows.
Don't worry: there are offers worse than dying.
There is the promise of more snow.
There is another storm to get things moving.

November Hunters

Winter fields are blank, cleared of all humanity
but wind, a muscle in the current
that draws geese in. The hunters crouch

in a low meadow, camouflaged by slush
and late weeds shooting through the frozen ground.
Guns uncased and leveled on their shoulders,

they wait for the Indian-cry of pintails,
war calls in the sky, to split their nerves open.
It isn't hunger that sends them out

in the muck and sludge. It isn't some
poverty in the blood that keeps them squatting
when their legs go numb. It's the pulse

of a gunshot strumming through the fingers,
how it yanks the shoulder back.
It's the moment a goose stalls

in mid-stroke and becomes a little tumbler,
the fluttering down that can make a heart
let go, then fill a chest with feathers.

Winter Farm

In the first half-sleep past the equinox,
you dream the babble of crows,
their furious tar, and clouds brooding
over the failed marriage of winds.
You wake with the hatching
shadows, sun pitched two steps
above the trees. If snow checked in,
a gathering of cattle. If not,
coyotes rove the fence-line.

Your ghost hands, your father's wards,
shiver with the memory of frost,
your first winter here, naming the ice.
The river spilled its voice in a tepid year
and now your trust in seasons drifts—
snow burns away by noon after Christmas
and hay wheels freeze up in June.

You cannot translate the language
of crows, or set the compass of weather
straight. Each year, when the grass refills
with color, a ghost flies free from each
of your hands. That morning you listen
for rain softly replacing itself on the roof,
or the confession a river makes across stones.

Zinnias

Every spring their orange
   arrows appear not far
      from my house, just far enough
       so my legs ache by the time I see them
    tearing apart the seams of their petals
      for the first time, cracking
       a cold fist where they've gripped
         all winter a clean and musical scent.
Every spring they stand,
   plain faced and honest,
      emptying their refineries
      of sweetness into the air,
   and I stand, legs aching,
      and think about how we come to trust such
      the stars will hatch into the sky every night,
         our bodies will remember the paths
     into and out of sleep, the spring
      currents will follow the first goose
        north, and these flowers will resume
           giving their fire away.

Walking Fields at Night
South of Hampton, Iowa

The last of the wheat is drought-bruised, bending
to its toes. Hay knuckled under weeks ago.

In the ditches, the hens form rows. Above me,
stars burn away the edges of quiet.

Gulls nest in grain elevators, hollow as sky,
when clouds don't keep a dark horizon.

I've walked a very long time, waiting to connect
these things to my life. Waiting to say—

*my heart burns in its great quiet, or wheat bends
in its brittle body and I bend in mine.*

Whatever flattens these fields, though, has little
to do with grief. And I can't speak for hens,

to say—*hens think stars are the ghosts of grain.*
I say, if there were no stars, I would not miss them.

A Map of Six States

Minnesota

Its little chimney punching
into Canada-sky, this house
is full of water, frozen now,
so my boot-prints harden
in the snow, so lakes are fitted
with lids and we are grateful.
We shiver nights to keep
heat bills low, leave the faucet
open to guard against a freeze.

Our voices multiply into lousy
weather, snow plows scraping
the asphalt. From Pennsylvania
you write, *it's OK if you think
of leaving me.* You didn't know?
They shoot geese here for less.

Tonight, when our hands don't
make shapes on each other's
bodies, and even the interplay
of our voices has blown away,
we will curl ourselves around
invisible stones when we sleep,
leave the apple hanging always
a hand's length above our reach.

Iowa

Missouri's headstone.
Weather's back room,
where corn stalks rot
in their cocoons. Frost
turns the best fields comatose.

In a garden, clumsy with
the corpses of marigolds,
your mother loses herself to dusk.
With her hands, she makes
a small coffin for a locust,
heavy with petals, ice
preserving its shape, but lifeless.

Nothing washed away
your mother's borders:
not a phantom marriage,
the storm of divorce,
wind from five children.
All of this is sealed in her.
Dusk presses into her face, vermilion.

Illinois

There's no sound Chicago
hasn't thought of: it has planes
above our hotel, lifting brief
storms into the sky, subways turning
on mechanical arms as they rumble by,
throaty grind of engines, hysteria of footfalls,
the tripled voices: Spanish, Korean, jive.

But it's the muted voices
that rattle the breath from us,
the one not in your throat, but in your eyes,
smoke rings blown from no mouth,
when you say, "I don't want
to end up like my mother."

That sound belongs to us,
and a city the past
would build between us.

Indiana

Pocket in the Midwestern pants. Lake
Michigan's shadow turns the whole state
gray. Extra tooth in the grin
of states between us, widening the gap.

I hate it for that. But why not say
hinge that holds these states together,
elbow in the arm from me to you?

Board in the fence between. Necessary doorway.
Indiana, we love you. Now go away.

Ohio

In Cleveland, they measure time
by how long it takes wind to blow
the harbor home, the huge clock downtown

resting its arms for winter. We unpacked
our first reunion here, snow powdering
the windows: four days, Thanksgiving, 1997.

In that hotel room, we measured time
our own way: not by the flow of minutes,
the bathtub filling and emptying of them,
but by their retreat from the rigged star
of our leaving, the shore coming out
to collect our rented boat.

Pennsylvania

Four-sided sea, where wide
sky and clouds mean
equally rain. Eastern moon,
so lazy it hasn't grown past
childhood, girl your mother
was, now lost between phases.
What is longing but the hatred of time?
In a poem for your mother, *the heart
is always lying. I say,* the heart
is lazy. On its pillow of muscle,
it taps itself to sleep. We need to
wake it with our curses—
shabby drummer, punching bag—
and feed its four mouths defeat.

We write poems because we can't
live the way we want, because
our heart-clocks are flawed.

They measure time by punching
at nothing, with the hope
there will be something there.

Tonight, I practice your face
in every vacancy—deep hat,
gaps my boot-prints crush
into the snow. The bells
at Lake Minnetonka,
their notes hollowed by cold,
chime out a funeral of hours.

In Lewisburg, you cook dinner
alone: cheese omelet with western potatoes.
You chop the moon-face of an onion
into smaller and smaller bits,
heavy knife signaling on the cutting board:
now now now now

(For Kathy Murphy)

Anna Anderson

Schizophrenic moon,
half-lit and fat with gravity,
wakes up the Princess in me.
I have the ghost of a girl
locked inside. I raise her in my mind,
the royal orphanage.

Daddy? They filled his chest
with notes, an eight beat scale
along the ribs.
From the mess he made,
I'd guess they played an aria.
And the little girl too,
dimpled with steel.

Now, when the Princess
puts my face on,
I'm one part nanny, one part brat.
And the moon—she wants me
to put rouge on it,
dress its dead face up.
I have no fools, no wizards
to quiet her. I do
what I can do—to shut her up,
I dance her around the room.

Muhammad Ali

In my gloves there is a place
for two small gods to live.
Right is Allah. Left, suffering.
I swing, left then right. Without
suffering there can be no Allah.
Left is past. Right is future.
My right hand seeks forgiveness
for my left hand's rage.

Edward at Maggie's Saloon

He's got little soldiers in the eyes,
bullets spinning through his mind.
The sky's an infirmary:
stars sweat their fevers out.
Their light floods the path
a bullet made, cools his dream
of cabins by the lake, long strings
of walleye, and a woman, early forties
and blonde, with eyes he could
drop an anchor into.

With the two-sided logic of a man
who has married his own misery,
he drinks so he can love,
brandy scouring his skull,
burning open his voice
until his heart is an orphanage
for the illiterate and inept, the dead
or near dead. Night pours out
into bourbon cups, shot-glasses
full of darkness, in which
his Adam's apple leaps.

Walter Mondale at McDonald's

He seems to hover above the strict geometry of tiles,
as I stand exposed in my no-brain crimson hat,
shirt ironed and tucked, almost, I fear, Republican.
I'm sixteen, running-mate to Mondale in my dreams.

How can he, the Midwest's JFK, getting ready,
I'm sure, to trounce Reagan in the next election,
drink the same vanilla shakes I drink on break?

And why does he not intercede when my manager
steers me out of the way, so she can take his order?
It's an act of subterfuge, an open political scandal!

A year later, Minnesota and I sit anchored
in an ocean of red, guarding our Democratic blue
as the states gang up against Mondale,
muscling him into a before-dinner concession.

When he congratulates Reagan, a fever
doesn't wash through his face. But he suckles on his lips
a little, like he's hungry, like someone put a Big Mac
down in front of him, and when he opened
the styrofoam lid, the box was empty.

Wal-Mart Sestina

Saturday mornings, they drive to Wal-Mart, usually
        through the rain,
the road a wrinkled sleeve in the windshield. Deserted carts,
miles from their corrals, fill the wind's shopping list:
        thousand drops of water,
half-pound fallen leaves. The entire parking lot serves
        as a filing cabinet,
cars carelessly indexed in their stalls, alphabetized
only by arrival. Is it wrong that they find comfort in commerce,

in merry-go-rounds of dresses, TVs flickering commercials,
synchronized so that when the penguin uncoils its rain-
bow of Froot Loops an entire wall becomes alphabetized
by color? Most days they are content to fill their cart
with simple things: shampoo, socks, paper lining
        for their cabinets.
Some days they leave having bagged only a jug of bottled water.

When they climb into his van, they pass the water
between them, taking drawn-out drinks usually seen
        in commercials.
All week in their apartment, they open and close cabinets,
the contents suddenly as appealing as another rainy
weekend. At night, he sneaks away to play darts
at the local bar, leaving her in bed, not sleeping,
        but alphabetizing

her daydreams. *A* is not for *anniversary*, but for *abatement*.
B is not *baby*. It's *bus-ticket*. She works as a waiter
so he can go to school and concentrate on his art,
a book of poems on the American addiction to commerce.

She takes long walks after work on days it doesn't rain,
and he frets for his supper, sulking in his hunger,
            slamming cabinet

doors. Even on her walk she feels him circle her, like a net
tossed from his voice, his useless logic in the wind,
            alphabetizing
her thoughts. She feels his eyes, cold as fall rain
on her skin. Later, she sinks into a warm bathtub, the water
holding her body together, while he pontificates on commerce,
drawing a metaphor between a stroller and a shopping cart,

unconcerned that some Saturdays his own shopping cart
blooms styrofoam and plastic, licorice, hair-gel, a cabaret
of corn chips and baseball cards, unwilling to admit his own
            love for commerce,
its ownability, each product in its ordered place, utterly
            alphabatizable.
And for her, Wal-Mart is a miracle of brightness, the aisles
            flooding not with water,
but with six kinds of Kool-Aid, sugarless canals, where
            together they drain,

dizzy and rain-less, cart swerving through that obstacle-
course of commerce, towards anything still new: a Water Pik,
a radio, or a filing cabinet where later she will alphabetize
            his poems.

For the Good Counsel Nun,
Who Left Her Brain to Science

When the Alzheimer's came to call,
when it entered her
like the Holy Spirit, when the doctor
explained adipose tissue, the five
islands of the brain, and the maps
he'd make of them, she didn't know
what was being asked, but she did
as she was trained: lifted
a smile to her ringed face
and signed her name.

Now, the whole church gossips
about the sister's brain, how it was unpacked
from its nest of bone, and pickled,
maybe, in the juices from a leftover
prayer, and how the stem of the spine,
rooted deep in the body,
held on to its missing bulb. The doctor,
they say, slices the frontal
lobe, thin as wafers from a loaf of bread.
He traces each weaved thought,
the entire mess of wires
that was her consciousness.

No one talks about the vacant
skull, empty now as the communion
cup, once the wine's all tasted
by the serious mouths. Only the altar
boy, the one who likes to clown

behind the father, claims
to have seen the famous brain,
soaking in formaldehyde
like a pair of dirty socks, crumpled
and rotating slowly in its jelly jar,
doing as the nun was trained: turning away
from the reflection in the glass.

Playing Yorick

For the actor who left his skull to the theater, to be used
in performances of Hamlet.

Dying? That's a matter of wardrobe,
an undressing, the easier
part of the role. What the audience wants
is a droll nod, a phantom smirk
where my chin cracked away.
Not the skull, but the face
that revolves around the skull,
Hamlet and I in a stare-down.

Night after night, the actor
lifts me like a waiter
clearing plates, an empty soup bowl
turned over on the tray.
Only the details change—light
funnels through my sockets
at a slower pace, my pose
skewed on the actor's palm,
his voice trembling off-key,
a fresh audience shuffled into the seats,

their faces like a jumble of scraps.
Only, more precise than that,
tailored almost, each one
a million tiny alterations from the last.
Hamlet offers me up to them
as a foreshadowing, a sample
of what's to come, an hors d'oeuvre.

The Block Party at The End of The World

On my second lap around the buffet,
it's hard to deny the appeal
of the arch-angel pie. And the bowl
of red beets could be our final communion—
one part wafer, one part wine.
But the only signs I see are the man
stirring the charcoal into flames, passing judgment
on the burgers and steaks, and the sunset
swirled into a young girl's hair, her lips
stained from a blast of atomic Kool-Aid.

Sometimes, the apocalypse doesn't
come. And if all the lawn chairs collapse
in the shade, if the cold chicken with coleslaw's
gone, the trinity of fork, knife and paper-plate
blown away, our desire for the end
of the world is still only the desire
to be close to each other, bravely sentimental
in our good-byes, the sky peeled back
like tinfoil from a pan.

Listen, I don't know much
about the world. But even I can see
the underground coils of grass,
the scaffolding for the future
already assembled beneath us,
bone-hard and merciless, and rising
through the interlocking path of our footprints.
Even I can see the paperboy
weaving his bike trail from doorway to doorway,
delivering the clear, devastating headline—
Anonymous Source Claims: We Are All Still Here

The Romanian Poet
(For Liliana Ursu)

Because she was not born into English, and because
she is alone tonight, she flattens her journal,
fat with nouns and busy with verbs.
On her lap, she writes:
The heron rearranges its feathers.
The moon keeps a curfew over the city.

Curfew— she's never used that word before.
She traces its loops:
the stone *C* curls itself around,
the depths of the *u*, little diver,
how *r* reaches into the back of *f*,
the double chin on the *e*,
and the *w*, spreading its wings
as if it could lift this word from the paper.

She loves the way the lean creek,
muscled between the streets
outside her apartment, hides the sound of an ocean
in a wave, and how all of language
comes stumbling from a single word.

She opens her window and sings *curfew, curfew, curfew*,
calling the night into her small room.

About the Author

Photo by Kathy Murphy

STEVE GERHKE graduated from the creative writing program at Minnesota State University in Mankato. He has received a fellowship to study at Bucknell University and a James Michener Fellowship from the University of Texas at Austin. He was a 1999 finalist for a Ruth Lilly Fellowship from *Poetry* magazine. He has worked as an editor on *Mankato Poetry Review* and *The Correspondent: A Fan Letter on Minnesota Writers.* Individual poems have appeared in *Midwest Quarterly, Chiron Review, Passages North, Flyway, South Dakota Review,* and the anthology *American Poetry: The Next Generation* (Carnegie Mellon University Press).